Practical

WILDFLOWER
GARDENING

YVONNE REES

The Crowood Press

First published in 1994 by
The Crowood Press Ltd
Ramsbury, Marlborough
Wiltshire SN8 2HR

British Library Cataloguing-in-Publication Data

A catalogue record for this book is available from the British
Library.

ISBN 1 85223 778 3

Acknowledgements

Picture Credits
All photographs by J.W. Kerswell except for those on pages 1,
2/3, 4, 7, 13 (both), 16, 17, 21, 22, 35, 42, 43, 48, 53, 55, 56
(both), 58, 59 (both), 62 and 63 which are by the author.
Line-drawings by Claire Upsdale-Jones.

Typeset in Optima by Chippendale Type Ltd,
Otley, West Yorkshire
Printed and bound by Paramount Printing Group, Hong Kong

CONTENTS

INTRODUCTION

Growing wild flowers in our own gardens not only provides the pleasure of an enjoyable and attractive display, it can also offer the satisfaction of knowing we are playing some small part in the conservation and continuation of these delightful yet often endangered species.

Wild flowers are rarely bright and showy: you have to observe their delicate blooms at close quarters or view them *en masse* to appreciate them fully. Even with exotic plants like orchids the colours and forms are subtle. However, where a single flower might be lost, the carpet effect of many plants strengthens the shade and can produce a stunning display. You will also find that a mixed planting of flowers of different species in varying colours naturally looks good, and you can create a pleasant

Wildflower plants are best grown in clumps of several plants to maximize the effect of flowers and foliage.

harmony without having to worry about clashing colours: consider, for example, the

Once established, a wild meadow requires far less maintenance than a formal clipped lawn and is more colourful. You can sow a small patch of flowery grass in any size plot, but this is an especially useful way of dealing with a large piece of land.

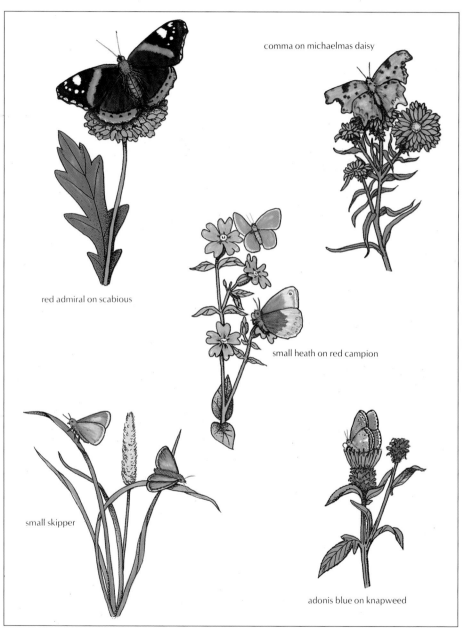

comma on michaelmas daisy

red admiral on scabious

small heath on red campion

small skipper

adonis blue on knapweed

You will find many new visitors to the garden if you can grow a few wild plants, particularly bees and butterflies looking for pollen and nectar.

wonderful multi-colour effect of an alpine meadow or the subtly contrasting colours and textures of a country hedgerow. Interestingly, you will find that many plants follow a kind of seasonal 'colour coding' anyway: a predominance of yellow flowering plants will appear in spring for example, giving way to the pinks and purples of summer, then autumn's russets, golds, reds and browns as seed heads and berries come into season.

The fact that many wild plants can appear a little unremarkable at first glance does not mean they have no place in our back yards and gardens. Even a patio tub or city window-box can offer an excellent environment for a few carefully chosen wild plants and bring a breath of the countryside to the most urban location. Once you have given the idea a little thought the possibilities are

endless: a wildlife pond, a natural hedge or an old stone wall make a fine feature within a more formal layout. If you have a larger patch to spare, you might even be able to create your own flowery meadow busy with bees and butterflies, or a small area of woodland, a haven to many birds and small mammals.

The beauty of many wild plants is that they are ideally equipped to cope with difficult conditions. There is always at least one or two you could grow in that dark and damp or dry stony corner where it may be hard to find a cultivated plant tough enough to survive, let alone give a good display. Shady parts of the garden can be real problem areas, particularly under trees and shrubs; but woodland plants are perfectly suited to this environment and can be most attractive, often growing quickly to create a

A selection of species trees, shrubs and plants will quickly attract a greater variety of insects and birds.

Even shady woodland areas come alive in spring with species daffodils and wood anemones.

dense carpeting effect which usefully suppresses weeds too. Alternatively, you might have a patch that is dry and stony – ideal for the kind of plants that grow on stone walls or rocky hillsides. A sandy soil might make an excellent environment for a selection of seaside plants, or a waterlogged area make a splendid bog garden.

With natural areas in the wild for such plants dwindling daily and increased general awareness that many wild plants – and the animals and insects that rely on them – are at risk of extinction, it has become much easier to acquire seeds and plants from specialist suppliers and even from your local garden centre, which has made planning and stocking a wildflower garden or feature much easier. Wildflower collections and seed mixtures are mostly sold according to their soil preference so that you can be sure you are sowing them in the right habitat. Conditions have to be just right for germination so you may need to be patient and wait for a frost or a hot dry spell to start the seed off. Waiting two years before you see results is common. Naturally it is no good planting a chalk-lover in a damp peaty soil and expecting it to flourish, so it pays to plan where your plants are going to grow and buy according to their

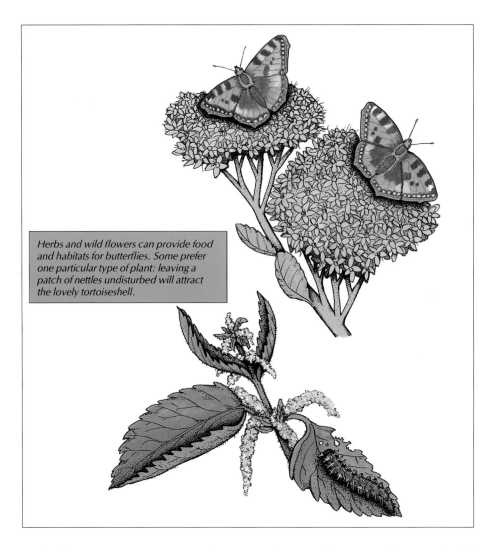

Herbs and wild flowers can provide food and habitats for butterflies. Some prefer one particular type of plant: leaving a patch of nettles undisturbed will attract the lovely tortoiseshell.

needs. You must never uproot your plants from the wild. Many are protected by law, although it is permissible to collect the seed of species not on the endangered list. Remember that just one flower head may yield hundreds of seeds so do not collect more than you need.

Another big advantage of growing wild plants in the garden is that even a small area or feature will attract a wide range of additional wildlife to your garden, from butterflies and bees to smaller insects and the birds and mammals that feed on them. You can encourage them further by providing a near-ideal habitat: plenty of cover for nesting species, sloping shallows to a natural pond to give easy access and the right kind of plants to provide nectar, nuts and berries.

1 • A WILDFLOWER FEATURE

If you would like to enjoy wild flowers from the privacy of your own back doorstep, you must decide how much space you can afford and the kind of feature that would be practical. It does not matter if you only have a small patio area or even a first-floor window-box – there are exciting ideas for all sizes and styles of garden, many of which are explored in more detail in Chapters 3 to 7. You may be prepared to transform the whole area into a wildflower garden or even be planning to purchase extra land for conservation purposes. Other factors will determine site and size: it may have to fit in with a more formal design for example, or you may have a problem area, such as a shady spot under trees or a boggy corner, which requires special treatment. Do you want your wildflower area to be visible from the house or a surprise feature to be discovered as you turn a corner, or partly concealed by hedges or trellis?

When you have decided where you would like your wildflower garden to be, the type of plants and style of feature you might plan will probably suggest itself. A damp hollow would make a wonderful pond or bog garden perhaps; or a large lawn you are fed up with mowing twice a week in summer could easily be converted in whole or part into a miniature wildflower meadow. The important thing is to choose the right kind of plants for the soil type and sun/shade conditions of your site so that they will thrive. To get your wildflower feature looking absolutely natural and right, your best bet is to go out into the country-side and look at similar spots in the wild: study the way a stream curves, how a pond is shaped or the kind of plants and flowers you find in a hedgerow.

Small Features

If you have only a limited space to spare for wild plants, or even if you barely have a

There are wild plants that will tolerate deep shade, like the unusual cuckoo pint, sometimes called lords and ladies (Arum maculatum), which produces curious fleshy green flowers – seen here about to unfurl – in spring.

garden at all – perhaps a tiny courtyard, a balcony or terrace – there are still many wonderful ideas you can adapt in miniature to enjoy a little of the sight and sensation of wild flowers. Consider the Japanese tradi-tional gardens for example: wonderful natu-ral landscapes in miniature with stones, sand and water used to represent moun-tains, lakes and beaches. Such schemes have a sense of tranquillity and offer hours of restful contemplation – a real asset in today's stressful times.

You can scale down your wildflower aspirations into tubs and containers for the patio, roof-garden or balcony. Plant these up with different grasses, wild herbs and

Pretty cornflower (*Centaurea cyanus*) with its spiky blue flowers and light narrow leaves was once a common sight for several summer months in the grain fields, but with stringent weed control these days it is more commonly seen in sunny grass areas and in our gardens. The wild plant is a self-seeded annual growing about 80cm (31.5in) high, but there is also a perennial cornflower (*Centaurea montana*) about 60cm (23.5in) high. This was originally introduced as a garden plant but it has moved the other way – escaping into the wild to grow along road-sides and on waste ground.

smaller wild flowers such as cornflowers or bugle. A tub, barrel or old sink might equally well be converted into a miniature wildlife pond. Make sure the container is watertight, then fill with water and add a few aquatic plants – many have tiny leaves and flowers ideal for this kind of treatment (although their growth habit can be vigorous and plants will need to be kept in check); there are even miniature water-lilies available.

To convert an old enamel sink or trough into a suitable container for a miniature alpine garden you can key the shiny surface with adhesive then press on a mixture of peat, sand and cement. Good drainage is important for rock-loving plants so place approximately 5cm (2in) of small stones or gravel in the bottom of the sink, then a layer of turf or moss to prevent the water from running through too quickly. Top up with a

Your wildflower feature need not take up a lot of space. Here wild plants have been used to soften the edges of a flight of informal stone garden steps.

If you have no room for wild flowers in the garden, grow them in individual pots and containers in the back yard and position them close together to achieve a countryside effect.

soil-based potting compost and position a few large stones or rocks on top for your plants to nestle between realistically. There are many miniature alpines to choose from so it really is a matter of personal choice.

A container as small as a window-box can be a haven for smaller, low-growing field and woodland species such as pansies and toadflax; you might even plant a selection of traditional meadow plants and a handful of grass seed which will attract bees and butterflies however urban the location.

Out in the garden, for those who are short of space or who want to hand over only a small area to nature, why not dedicate a small island bed or raised bed to wild plants? This would help to keep them contained. Alternatively, you might prefer to blur the edges between formality and informality: in this case, an area of longer, flower-planted grass might be part of a larger, smarter lawn. Providing your wild area is not likely to be walked on continuously like other parts of the lawn you

Wildflower features can sit happily alongside more formal parts of the garden if you design them carefully. A smartly mown sward might border a more unkempt wildflower meadow, for example.

should be able to cultivate a splendid display of buttercups, daisies and clover simply by not mowing it. Other flowers can be seeded there if you wish: blue speedwell, bright poppies or ragged robin. A small bog area or natural pond always fits well with more formal features and can be linked to the main garden by natural and often dramatic water's-edge plants. Once you start exploring the possibilities they seem endless: a meandering stream used to divide the garden into more interesting shapes and sections; an informal path or flight of steps linking one area to another and planted with carpet-forming wild flowers and herbs like thyme or woodruff; an otherwise unattractive bank of earth, seeded with

grass and meadow plants such as lady's bedstraw, cowslips and ox-eye daisies.

If you have trees or shrubs in the garden, make the most of woodland flowers by planting a selection of woodland ground-cover plants such as celandines, ground ivy and cyclamen in the shady areas where little else might grow. Depending on how much space you have, you could even create a tiny woodland in miniature using a few of the smaller species of trees or a selection of shrubs in conjunction with ground-cover plants such as these. Another small-space wildflower idea is to plant upwards rather than outwards: a simple framework or trellis need only take up a few feet of space but might be planted with the

One of the most delightful woodland plants to flower in spring is the wood anemone (*Anemone nemorosa*) whose delicate white blooms shine out in shady grass and brushwood areas. Sometimes known as the windflower, the wood anemone is a common perennial plant, growing to approximately 30cm (12in). The celery-like foliage is as attractive as the flowers, which might be pink or purple as well as white. The plant is poisonous.

most beautiful wild climbers for a fabulous informal display of scented honeysuckle or showy *convolvulus*.

On a Larger Scale

If you have more space to spare you can really introduce a slice of countryside into the garden, a place where you might slip away to relax and breathe in subtle scents and colours, maybe even to take a picnic and pretend you have travelled miles away from home. You can buy meadow grass and flower-seed mixtures quite easily for making a wildflower 'meadow' – this could be as large or as small as you wish. Once the plants have established themselves you could not ask for a more delightful, easy-to-maintain feature. The area will need cutting only once a year – in summer for a

Woodland plants are perfect for shady areas with a rich moist soil.

If space is limited or you prefer a more formal style garden, you could always create a relaxing wildflower corner where plants could be contained, and where you might sit and enjoy them at leisure.

spring-flowering meadow or in autumn for a late summer-flowering one. This cut is generally done by hand using a scythe. As with any wildflower feature, good preparation is essential to remove any weeds and create a suitable environment for your wild plants; this is covered in more detail in Chapter 3 (*see* page 23).

Your main beds and borders can offer equally good opportunities for creating a wildflower display. Providing you take the trouble to plan it carefully at the outset, there could be something of interest right through the year. Bulbs are a wonderful mainstay, providing colour at the earliest times of the year and maintaining a fine display until the first summer blooms appear: avoid the showy hybrid types and plant simple snowdrops, species daffodils and crocuses. Most of the specialist bulb catalogues can offer a small selection of species bulbs many of which, particularly the tulips, are delicate but delightful. Remember to plant your bulbs in drifts or random blocks for the most natural effect. Later in the year you can enjoy a mass of brilliant poppies, ox-eye daisies, spreading crane's-bill and many other lovely wild flowers that will do well in a sunny bed or border. Leave these to self-seed and your display will be even better the following year. A selection of evergreen creepers and

Where you want to make a path through or near a wildflower feature, choose an informal style such as stone, gravel or bark chips.

climbers like ivy, or berried plants like buckthorn, will maintain interest in autumn and winter.

One of the most spectacular and easy-to-establish wildflower features is a pond or marsh; if you do have the space to install a good-sized one you will be well-rewarded with a fine natural-looking feature and an excellent selection of wild water-loving plants within two years, even if you don't bother to plant anything yourself. A natural water feature has the added advantage that it attracts a wide range of wildlife such as frogs, newts, dragonflies and other insects as well as birds. If excavating a large area is not practical, a damp marshy spot offers equal scope for an impressive range of bog plants like the giant-leaved gunnera or the delicate fritillary.

Once installed, a pond or marsh requires very little maintenance and since the plants are most vigorous growers, it does not take long to establish itself. A natural hedgerow takes a little more time and patience, but if you are looking for a boundary or screen to suit an informal or cottage garden, or if you are interested in preserving the traditional habitat of a great many small mammals and birds, you can choose nothing better. You will need plenty of space as little else will grow in the shade of the immediate surroundings; a wild hedgerow will also need to be kept free from weeds and trimmed regularly until it is established.

A wildlife pond is simple to install and once established requires very little maintenance. It is the perfect opportunity to grow an interesting selection of lush pool-side plants.

The dogrose (*Rosa canina*) is one of the most beautiful hedgerow and woodland plants, reaching a height of around 3m (9ft) and covering a tree or hedge with a mass of beautiful blooms. The fragrant flowers can vary greatly in appearance, coming in many different forms and shades of pink and white. It is a perfect climber for the informal garden, the stunning yet delicate blooms showing well against the bright green leaves. When the flowers have finished the plant produces a superb display of bright red hips which are very attractive to birds.

Unless you are lucky enough to have a selection of trees already established in your garden, time and patience will also be required to create an effective woodland garden: this could take rather less space than you might think and with careful planning may be fitted effectively into a typical long, narrow suburban back garden. In this case, however, you must turn the whole area over to this one feature and add shade-loving woodland plants to provide ground cover.

If you love alpine plants and have the space, it might be worth creating a large rock garden or alpine bank, which is also a useful way to cope with a change of level within the garden, or to add height and variety to your general scheme. Where this might not be practical, use those wild flowering plants that prefer a dry, stony environment for easy-care gravel beds, old stone walls and the cracks around and between the slabs in a paved area.

2 • BUYING AND PROPAGATING PLANTS

Wild flowers will grow well in most garden conditions from tubs to borders – once they have established themselves and if they are given suitable conditions. You must not expect to propagate and grow wild plants as readily as today's highly bred varieties although there are many well-known 'weeds' that take some stopping! The secret really is patience and a good basic knowledge of each plant's particular needs.

Buying Wildflower Plants

Wildflower plants are more readily available these days thanks to a greater demand from discerning gardeners. It is important that you do not collect plants from the wild without a proper licence (and this applies world-wide). Collecting seed or swapping plants with like-minded friends is by far the

To position a pot-grown plant, dig out a hole slightly bigger than the rootball of the plant, lower it gently into the hole making sure it stands straight, and backfill with soil, firming as you go.

Unfortunately, cowslip makes an excellent wine, which has made it rare where once it was common, flowering in spring along the grassy banks and in the meadows of England, Wales and central Ireland. The flowers, so like a bunch of golden keys, hang from long stems above thick felt-like leaves, making it an attractive and easily identified species. Cultivated plants are easily obtained from specialist nurseries who may have it listed under *Primula veris* – its Latin name. Cowslips are perennial plants that love chalk, but will also do well in clay or damp soils. They will grow to around 30cm (1ft).

better option from a conservation point of view. It is illegal to uproot any wild plant. Check the protected list on page 61 for plants that must not be disturbed in any way whatsoever.

You will find a good range of wildflower plants and plantlets at specialist nurseries and at herb nurseries. Some operate a mail-order system which is useful if there is no nursery in your area. Buying individual plants is a good idea if you only want one or two for a small feature, as growing from seed always produces rather too many specimens. Growing from seed takes longer too – ready-grown plants are perfect for an almost instant effect.

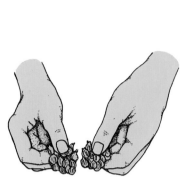

You can gently separate the tiny bulbils that form around the base of bulb-producing plants and use them to grow new plants.

Softwood cuttings can be taken from woody perennial plants in the summer to propagate new plants.

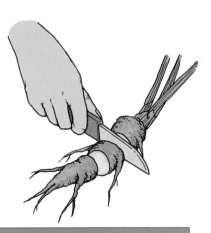

Root cuttings are made by slicing off a thick section of root that includes a healthy bud.

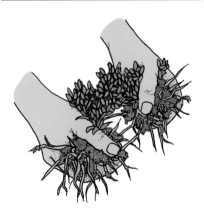

Lift clump-forming plants in autumn and gently prise them apart into smaller clumps to make new plants and revive the old.

Methods of propagation.

Layering and Cuttings

Another option if you don't want to grow plants from seed is to propagate new plants from your own or a friend's existing stock. This is particularly effective when propagating plants that put out runners like yellow archangel and bugle. It is also a practical alternative for those plants that broadcast their seed via nature's own trigger system, which makes them difficult to collect: violets and crane's-bill are examples. Stems of vigorous plants can be pegged down onto the soil and the new plants removed from the parent only when they have rooted. Other plants like lady's-smock can be propagated from leaf cuttings; others can be simply divided to make new plants, for example primroses and cowslips.

Propagating from Seed

Growing your own plants from seed is relatively inexpensive and provides plenty of plants for larger features or to exchange with like-minded friends. The cheapest option of all, of course, is to collect your own seed, and this can be done from the wild providing you don't touch any of the plants on the endangered species list. This list is being updated all the time, so always check it before you go collecting to ensure that the species you require has not been added to it.

You will need to know the best time to collect the seed from any specific plant as it must be captured just as it ripens: that is, when the seed head has dried out and gone brown. Seeds should not be green or moist. You will need a paper bag to collect your seeds, never a plastic one because these develop moisture and can cause the seeds to go musty. Plants may need a paper bag tying over the head of the flower in order to catch the seeds as they are ripened and broadcast. Some are quite easy to collect providing the day is not a windy one – dandelions and cowslips for example. Others, like poppies, have to be tipped up

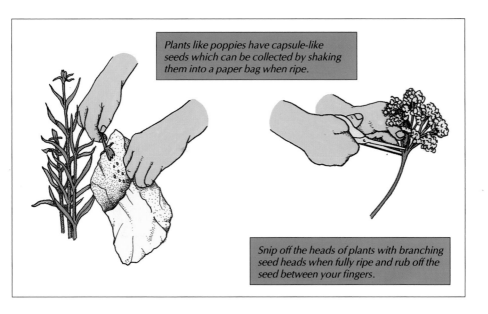

Plants like poppies have capsule-like seeds which can be collected by shaking them into a paper bag when ripe.

Snip off the heads of plants with branching seed heads when fully ripe and rub off the seed between your fingers.

Capsule-forming plants tip their seeds onto the ground below, where it is an easy job to collect the seedlings once they have germinated.

Some species like dandelions produce fluffy seed heads which are designed to be wind-borne. To collect them before they are dispersed you will have to pull off the individual 'parachute' seeds and store in a paper bag.

Plants such as meadow crane's-bill incorporate a kind of trigger system which catapults the seeds away from the plant. This makes the seed difficult to collect; to catch it when it is really ripe, tie paper bags over the heads of the flowers before they are fully ripe, snip them off and ripen in a container covered with muslin to prevent the seeds escaping.

Agrimony has an interesting way of dispersing its seed: the seed heads are prickly so they catch on the fur of passing animals.

Methods of seed dispersal.

to examine the seed which is enclosed in a capsule.

Some seeds you will be happy for the plant to broadcast itself and encourage new plants next season. Others you will be keen to propagate yourself. Store excess seed in vacuum-sealed plastic sandwich boxes in the refrigerator at a temperature of around 2°C (36°F) making sure the boxes are well-labelled. These should keep indefinitely. Silica packets (available from chemists) will prevent the seeds from becoming damp and mouldy.

Sowing Techniques

Some wildflower plants such as marsh and woodland species are quite difficult to propagate from seed. Others, like the meadow flowers, are relatively easy: corn cockle and corn marigold can be up and flowering within a matter of months. Generally speaking wild plants are used to struggling against the odds; they may just take a little longer to germinate than you might expect, so don't give up too soon.

Seed is best sown in raised seed beds but if you do not have room for a nursery corner in your garden they can be grown in seed-trays or sown directly into the ground.

Sowing Seeds in Seed Beds

A permanent area where seeds of wild plants might be sown – a kind of nursery bed tucked away in a corner of the garden – is ideal as you are less likely to get impatient waiting for seeds to germinate and throw them away; this also solves the problem of what to do with biennial species such as foxgloves and mullein. The area will need to be thoroughly cleared of any existing perennial weeds such as dock and nettle, then raked and rolled until a fine tilth is achieved. Sow seed in drills, cover lightly and net against birds.

A handsome deciduous shrub, Broom (*Cytisus scoparius*, also *Sarrothamnus scoparius*) smothers its long, narrow branches in golden flowers in early spring. The flowers are followed by fine black seed pods. In the wild, broom is common on heaths and waste ground; in the garden it would suit a sunny border where, given ideal conditions, it grows to around 2.5m (8ft). It does not grow very well in chalky soils. The plant was indeed once used for making brooms which is where it gets its common name.

Sowing Seeds in Trays

Propagating seeds in trays sometimes suits those plants that are difficult to germinate (like marsh plants) as the soil can be kept extra moist. Seed trays should be prepared by filling with a good gritty compost rather than a peat-based type; then seeds should be sown in autumn for germination the following spring. The trays can be watered with a fine rose and kept covered with a sheet of glass or an open-ended cloche to prevent rain and wind washing the seeds away, while still allowing the cold weather to do its work. Standing the trays on an old piece of carpet helps keep the soil moist.

Mixing wildflower seed with grass seed makes it easier to sow. Over large areas, divide the plot into more manageable sections and proportion the seed accordingly.

Sowing Seeds Directly into the Ground

Seed can be sown directly into the ground in spring or autumn depending on the plant species. It is important that the ground is weed-free and finely raked, so it will need some preparation beforehand, even if planting directly into a bed or border. If you are sowing a large area with a meadow mixture, you can estimate how much you need by using approximately 30g (1oz) per square metre (yard) for a grass and flower mixture; and 15–20g (½–¾oz) per square metre (yard) for flower seed alone. To make sure the seeds are scattered evenly clasp a small amount in your fist and swing your hand from side to side, allowing the seeds to slip through your fingers. After sowing, roll the area to press the seed into the soil then leave mother nature to do her work. There is no need to water.

One of our largest-leaved plants, *Gunnera manicata* grows as tall as 2m (6ft) with spectacular leaves 1.5m (5ft) across. It needs a sheltered site and damp soil and is most often seen growing at the edges of ponds or beside streams. The massive leaves make this an excellent plant for the garden and it is mostly grown as an architectural foliage plant although the strange green flower spikes which appear in early summer are also unusual. These are followed by orange-brown seed pods. The plant needs protection after it has died down for winter: usually, a couple of the large leaves are folded down over the crown.

Common Causes of Failure

● Soil is too rich.
● Bird damage: firm down soil and net to protect seeds.
● Slug damage to young plants.
● Seeds sown at the wrong time: wildflower seeds are best sown in autumn not spring. Many need the winter dormant phase to germinate. This can be done artificially by putting the seeds in the freezer at two day intervals – two days in then two days out. This process is called vernalization.

3 • A WILDFLOWER MEADOW

A lush meadow of long grass studded with wild flowers like an exotic colourful carpet is a rare sight these days. Not so long ago you could expect as many as 150 different species of plants in a meadow only a hectare (2 acres) square. Even a small patch one metre square would display a good thirty different plants. Sadly, modern farming methods and the widespread use of herbicides have virtually reduced this splendid sight to little more than a memory. This is why growing your own flowery meadow, however small, is of great importance to the survival of typical meadowland plants and the animals and insects which depend on them. If you do not have a spare acre or two, the smallest corner of the garden or even a window-box will give equal pleasure. If your planned wildflower garden is not contained in this manner but part of a larger, more formal layout, you will have to integrate it carefully with other features or it will look out of place. A pond

and marsh make good neighbours; or you could plan a small group of trees and shrubs, perhaps an informal hedge, to mark at least one of its boundaries.

You can buy the grass and flower seed ready mixed from garden centres, wildflower and herb stockists or via your local commercial seed suppliers. The mixture will be specially balanced to suit a particular location and soil type and will be formulated for spring or autumn flowering. You can mix your own selection by buying individual flowering species and adding them to a non-rye grass mix. Do make sure the flowers are suited to the same conditions.

Before you rush out enthusiastically and scatter the seed around in imitation of nature, take the time and trouble to prepare the proposed site carefully as this will ensure best results. A good rich soil is not really suitable as it feeds the grasses too well, so they tend to swamp the flowering

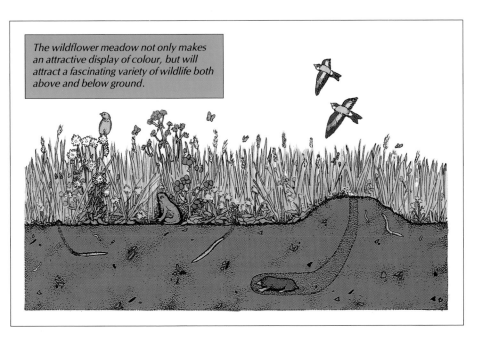

The wildflower meadow not only makes an attractive display of colour, but will attract a fascinating variety of wildlife both above and below ground.

plants: a thin sandy or lime soil is better. If your proposed site is a little too rich you can reduce its fertility by stripping off the turf and about 10cm (4in) of the topsoil. It is also important to ensure that the area is completely free of weeds, especially perennial weeds such as thistle and dock. If you have the patience, close mowing over several seasons using a grass box to remove the clippings should produce results without the use of chemicals. Otherwise, it is a case of hand weeding and digging out the roots, which is only really practical for small areas, or using a perennial non-persistent weed-killer.

Flowers in Your Lawn

Providing you have not used weed-killer on

The humble daisy can transform a simple area of grass into a star spangled carpet providing you don't keep cutting off the flower heads with your lawnmower.

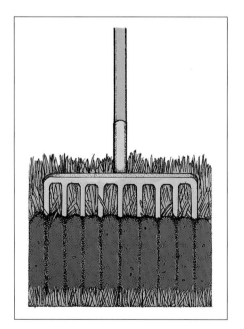

An existing patch of grass must be scarified or raked to expose patches of bare soil before sowing wildflower seed.

your grass for the last couple of years, you could encourage a crop of wild flowers such as daisies, dandelions, clover and cow parsley in your lawn simply by not mowing the grass until summer. You can start mowing again when the flowers are finished to regain a more conventional turf. A spring display is equally easy to achieve by planting bulbs in the grass in autumn. For the most natural effect, plant the less showy species of daffodils, narcissi, snowdrops and crocuses in large groups or bands. Avoid small clumps of flowers and plant as many as you can afford for a massed effect. You can plant bulbs quickly using a special tool; or remove a section of turf, plant a group of bulbs then press back into position. If you let the foliage die back naturally and allow the flowers to set seed, the bulbs should naturalize and maintain an even better display in later years. Try to leave the grass unmown until early summer; you may like to leave a path through the flowers which can be mown for easier access to the rest of the garden.

Converting Your Existing Lawn

You can convert your striped green sward into a lovely flowery meadow quite easily. Stop applying fertilizer straight away and lift the turf to remove a layer of topsoil as described on page 24. Don't waste the valuable nutrients but use this elsewhere in the garden. To introduce wild flowers into the grass, you should cut it back as low as possible in spring or autumn and rake to

remove any loose grass. On a fine day you can rake the seed into any bare areas of earth, roll and water lightly. You will have to cut the grass every six to eight weeks in the first year using the mower blades at their highest level. Ideally the plants should be left around 7–10cm (3–4in) tall which will encourage root growth in your flowering plants while keeping the grass in check.

It is also possible to introduce flowers into your lawn using ready-established plants. This a practical option for smaller areas where you might only need a few species or where you are impatient for results and cannot wait anything up to two years for some species to germinate. Water

If you know someone who has an established wildflower meadow or lawn, you can successfully transfer a section by cutting and lifting the turf, and replanting it in its new site to spread and self-seed. This must never be done with plants in the wild.

both the plant and the ground before planting, dig a hole just a little larger than the rootball of the plant, lift it gently out of its pot and place the plant in the hole, spreading the roots out gently and backfilling with soil. The plant should be at the same level as it was growing at before. Firm well and water in.

Planting a New Flower Meadow

Once you have made sure your designated area is not too rich and is free of weeds, it should be thoroughly dug over, raked and rolled to create a fine tilth for your seeds. This should only be done in dry weather or the soil will become clogged. The seed should be broadcast evenly covering every square metre (yard) with approximately 30g (1oz) of seed. Mixing the seed with fine sand helps spread it more evenly. Autumn is the best time to sow as a spell of cold weather encourages germination in the spring. Otherwise, sow in early spring. Water with a fine rose and cut the area to a height of approximately 5–10cm (2–4in) every six to eight weeks to give the flowering plants a chance to grow. You will not see any blooms until the following year.

Mowing Flower Meadows

Flowery meadows still require mowing although this is far less frequent than for traditional lawns. However, it is important this is done correctly to achieve the right results. When you mow will depend on whether you are planning a spring- or summer-flowering area. If you are particularly keen to encourage wildlife such as butterflies, the area will have to be managed differently again: to ensure a good variety of habitats for different species, cut some areas but not others at different times

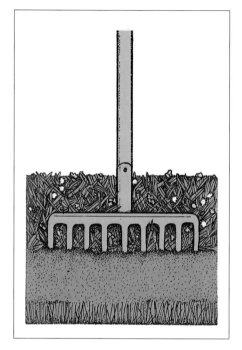

You must rake up the hay after mowing a wildflower meadow. This prevents it creating a mulch which will suppress your wildflower plants.

of the year. Give the whole area a final cut in autumn. You will not be able to use a conventional motor mower; an electric or petrol strimmer might be practical for small areas, otherwise it is down to muscle power and a hand scythe. Whatever routine you adopt, the area should be trampled after the main mow to press the seed into the ground – a job traditionally carried out by cattle.

Spring-Flowering Meadow

For a spring-flowering meadow, the grass will not be mown until midsummer giving the flowers time to finish and set seed. The meadow should be scythed or mown to a height of around 5–10cm (2–4in). Leave the hay for a couple of days to dry – this will depend on the weather – and turn it daily to encourage the seeds to fall. You must rake up the hay and remove it – use it as fodder if you have animals. For the rest of the year the area can be mown normally as required, and used as a conventional lawn, but you must make sure you remove all the grass cuttings and do not mow too close. Remember not to use any fertilizer or weed-killer.

Summer-Flowering Meadow

The summer-flowering meadow will have to be cut regularly from early spring to early summer taking care not to mow too low and kill the plants off altogether. Allow to flower and do not mow again until autumn when the flowers are finished and seed has been scattered naturally. Cut and dry the hay as for a spring-flowering meadow.

The wild candytuft (*Iberis amara*) is an annual cornfield plant which is also seen frequently on hillsides in southern areas of England. It prefers a dry calcareous soil and can make an attractive garden plant for dry stony areas. The stems of small white flower clusters grow to around 30cm (12in) high. Wild candytuft flowers for around eight weeks in summer.

Extremely common along roadsides, the bright perennial ox-eye daisy (*Leucanthemum vulgare* or *Chrysanthemum leucanthemum*) is another garden favourite, grown for its lovely display of daisy-like white flowers and small glossy leaves. The plants stand about 20–70cm (8in–2.5ft) high and are ideal for sunny borders, meadows or marsh areas where they will flower right through the summer.

Planting a Cornfield

Before the introduction of herbicides, the summer cornfields were a blaze of colour with wild flowers as well as golden wheat and barley. As long as your garden does not border grain fields – your local farmer probably won't be very happy if your flower seeds drift over – you can have a flowery field of your own. Cornfield seed mixes are available and these can be planted any-where from patio tub to two-acre field. The soil does not have to be impoverished in the same way it does for meadow mixes as there are no grasses to compete with, but you will have to prepare the soil and scarify it in some way in spring and autumn to encourage the seeds to germinate. An autumn sowing will produce results the next summer; sowing in early spring means the plants will flower in mid to late summer.

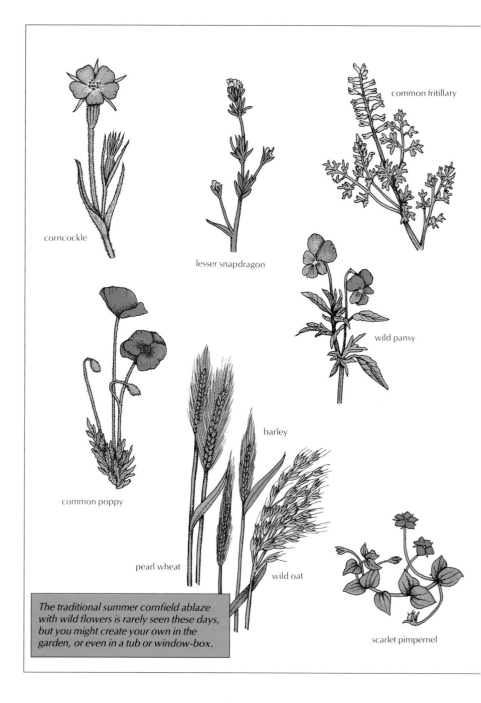

common fritillary

corncockle

lesser snapdragon

wild pansy

barley

common poppy

pearl wheat

wild oat

scarlet pimpernel

The traditional summer cornfield ablaze with wild flowers is rarely seen these days, but you might create your own in the garden, or even in a tub or window-box.

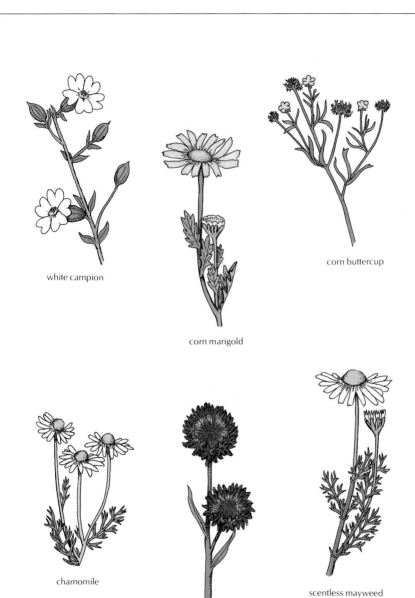

white campion

corn marigold

corn buttercup

chamomile

cornflower

scentless mayweed

4 • HEDGEROW PLANTS

A natural hedgerow does not just serve as a solid stock-proof boundary. It is a haven for a wide range of wildlife including birds and small mammals who rely on the hedge plants for food and shelter. An informal hedge is also an attractive feature, perfectly suited to a cottage-style property and providing something of interest virtually all the year round. A well-planned hedge might include a wide range of small trees, shrubs, climbers and wild flowers, yet take up a relatively small amount of space. What you grow will depend to some extent on where the hedge is to be positioned: remember that if it forms part of a boundary, you will only get the benefit of one side of it. A hedge running east–west will have an extremely sunny and a shady side; the ideal is a south-east–north-west hedge with your garden on the north-west side so that it receives some shade in the afternoons.

A Single-Species Hedge

A single-species hedge is not as varied nor as informal, but it can still be highly attractive; and if you don't prune it too seriously it will develop a shaggy, slightly rampant look that can be perfectly suited to less formal gardens and features. Letting shrubs and plants flower and fruit freely also allows birds to feed. Holly, barberry and *Pyracantha rogersiana* are attractive evergreens which also have bright berries; while dense yew grows so slowly it only needs cutting back annually. Individual plants should be positioned about 45cm (1½ft) apart and will have made a good mature hedge after about six years. Clip plants to a height of around 1.5m (5ft) to encourage nesting birds. Sweet-briar makes a lovely hedge with the advantage of beautiful pink blooms in summer and tasty hips in autumn. A

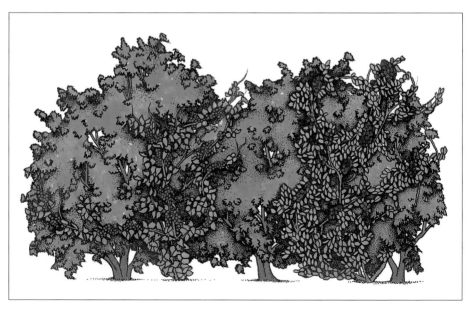

The natural hedgerow is made up of a wide selection of different plants, including shrubs, trees and climbers which grow together to create a colourful and interesting feature.

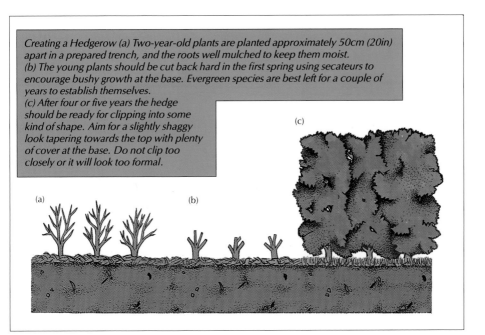

Creating a Hedgerow (a) Two-year-old plants are planted approximately 50cm (20in) apart in a prepared trench, and the roots well mulched to keep them moist.
(b) The young plants should be cut back hard in the first spring using secateurs to encourage bushy growth at the base. Evergreen species are best left for a couple of years to establish themselves.
(c) After four or five years the hedge should be ready for clipping into some kind of shape. Aim for a slightly shaggy look tapering towards the top with plenty of cover at the base. Do not clip too closely or it will look too formal.

hedge planted solely with beech or hornbeam can be clipped to give a slightly more formal appearance.

A Mixed Hedge

When choosing plants for a natural hedge, aim for a good variety of shapes and colours throughout the year. About 70 per cent will be hawthorn with its fresh green leaves (delicious between slices of bread and butter) creamy white flowers and red autumn berries. This is planted at regular intervals and grows thick and fast. Other plants to be inserted at random might include the pretty dogrose, sweet-scented honeysuckle, bronze-leaved field maple or climbing hops with their papery green cones. Other plants will grow in the difficult conditions at ground level without depriving the main hedge plants of valuable nutrients: cow parsley, hogweed and harebells in summer and creamy yellow primroses in spring.

Prepare the site by digging over and getting rid of any perennial weeds. A trench about 30cm (1ft) wide with plenty of well-rotted manure or leaf mould in the bottom will get your hedge plants off to a good start. Buy young bare-rooted specimens that will get away quickly and plant them in autumn or winter while the plants are dormant, watering well before planting. Shrubs and trees ought to be planted in two staggered rows approximately 15–20cm (6–8in) apart allowing 30cm (1ft) between the plants to encourage a good, thick hedge. If possible, plant in autumn, as the soil will still be warm from summer sunshine which will encourage the roots to grow. Water regularly to keep the roots damp or surround them with a thick mulch to help preserve moisture. This might be grass cuttings, bark chips, black polythene or even old pieces of carpet.

If there are a few gaps once the hedge is established, these can be filled with new seedlings, provided you feed them well to compensate for the greedy bigger plants.

Planting shrubs at an angle of around 45 degrees to the ground encourages new shoots to grow vertically and will produce a thick base to the hedge. Another way to encourage bushy growth and good root development is to prune back shrubs and trees to 15–20cm (6–8in). Should the hedge still look too gappy once it is starting to establish itself, gaps can be filled with new shrubs providing you give them extra nutrients as they will be competing with the established plants. Position your new plants in the trench as before, backfill with soil or better still, manure, firm in and water thoroughly.

Grass and under-hedge plants (also birds and small mammals such as hedgehogs, voles and shrews) usually appear spontaneously after several seasons; but if you want to introduce them yourself, pretty wild flowers like herb Robert, campion, bugle and St John's wort can be grown from seed or bought as plants. Most will grow well in the damp, shady conditions beneath a hedge, and are tolerant to most soils.

Pruning the Hedgerow

Hedgerow shrubs and trees will need a hard prune for the first two seasons to encourage bushy new growth. After that it will only be necessary to trim plants back once a year until they reach the required size. Trees are usually reduced to shrub size but you can leave the occasional specimen to add height and interest to the hedge and also to provide extra nectar, berries and nuts. Once the hedge is established an annual prune should suffice, preferably in early winter. Pruning in springtime removes flower buds and new leaf growth and disturbs nesting birds, while an autumn pruning removes valuable berries and other fruits. When pruning, aim at a sort of wedge shape, tapering towards the top of the stem to prevent snow resting on the top and causing damage.

The area below and around the hedge will need cutting down; late winter is probably the best time for this, before the first spring bulbs begin to appear. You can use a strimmer or a hand scythe for this job.

5 • WOODLAND WILD FLOWERS

Even if you have no room in your garden to create a mini woodland, there will surely be a place for the kind of plants that are specially adapted for the shady conditions on the woodland floor. Deep and partial shade are always tricky sites in the garden yet woodland species include some delightful and indeed quite beautiful wild flowers. Some will thrive in full shade; others prefer a dappled light or semi-shade. Use them to create a lovely wildflower area beneath a large existing tree where so far you have only been able to display bare earth. These species are perfect for those familiar problem areas: a shady area by the front door or in the corner of a patio; the tiny city back yard overshadowed by tall walls.

Trees and Shrubs

You may be lucky enough to own a garden or piece of land with existing mature trees and shrubs that simply need a little management or underplanting to transform them into a delightful woodland feature. Trees that have grown too tall can be coppiced (*see* page 37). A dense group may need thinning by taking out the weakest specimens or the whole area can be livened up by the introduction of a few new species, perhaps to add something of interest through the seasons: spring blossom, winter berries or autumn foliage. A few evergreen specimens are always useful to provide substance in the winter. Old trees and other less attractive features may be smothered in woodland climbers such as honeysuckle, white bryony or traveller's joy.

If you have no existing trees and you have the patience to wait a few years before your plans begin to show signs of maturity, you can at least take pleasure in choosing a fine selection of native species to create a woodland area of your own design. If the area available is not large, choose the smaller species such as rowan, birch, elder, hazel

Garlic mustard (Alliaria petiolata) *looks fresh and lively, the small white flowers and bright green stems standing sentry in the woods or by the hedge – giving the plant one of its popular common names: Jack-by-the-hedge. The crushed leaves smell strongly of garlic.*

The curious looking toothwort (Lathraea squamaria) *is actually a parasite that grows on the roots of hazel. The strange fleshy flowers all face one way and stand about 30cm (12in) high. They are sometimes called corpse flowers.*

snowberry

holly

Trees and shrubs can offer the pleasure of seasonal fruits and berries, as well as their general shape and the colour and form of their foliage. These, together with the spring blossom and bark, will attract many insects and birds.

mountain ash

wild cherry

elder

and thorn. Avoid anything too ornamental or showy as it will only look out of place. Trees with striking foliage such as bronze or gold can also spoil a harmonious scheme so use these sparingly as a highlight or focal point.

It is a good idea to study the trees in your area to see which are particular to your climate and soil type before making your choice then to aim for a good variety of tree shapes and sizes within that range. Some species are columnar, for example: that is, they are tall and narrow, making them perfect for gardens with limited space or where you are looking to add a little height

*The hawthorn (*Crataegus monogyna*) or quickthorn is the main component of a natural hedgerow, but it also makes an excellent specimen tree for small gardens growing no taller than 8m (26ft). You may hear it referred to as the May-tree, because it is one of the first to green up into leaf after winter; the mass of snowy blossom has a strange musky scent.*

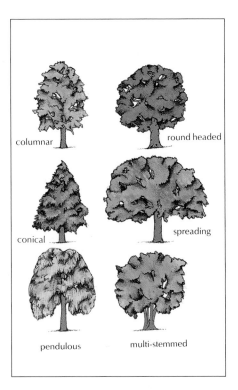

columnar

round headed

conical

spreading

pendulous

multi-stemmed

Trees and shrubs offer a wide variety of shapes and sizes that can be used to create an interesting group or landscape even if you have room only for a few specimens.

and elegance to your planting scheme. Other trees might be conical, weeping or round-headed. The leaves are all different too: they may be delicate and fern-like, large and glossy like giant hands or needle-thin like spines. There is plenty of scope to create interesting contrasts and harmonies. Do not group different types of tree together, however, as this would look unnatural. A clump of several trees of the same type can look highly attractive with perhaps a couple of different types just for contrast.

Trees always seem to look better grouped in odd numbers – threes or fives for example. Plant them at least 1–1.5m (3–5ft) apart to allow them to grow to their proper shape and to ensure the area beneath is not too shady. In a small garden it may be advisable to prune off the lower branches to a height of around 1.2–1.5m (4–5ft) while the tree is dormant (between the end of autumn and

A successful woodland creates a multi-layered effect, with a high canopy of large trees graduating down through smaller trees and shrubs to the shade-loving plants that flourish on the woodland floor.

early spring) to make a little more space between and beneath them.

Successful planting of these larger elements in the landscape relies on a three-tier approach. The tallest trees are your 'canopy': they are predominant and they shade the other plants. They are also useful for hiding an unwelcome view or eyesore. Below these is the 'understorey' of smaller tree species and shrubs, all of which must be able to tolerate the shade created by their taller cousins. Next comes a 'brush' level of smaller shrubs and creepers ending on the woodland floor; here a fabulous selection of woodland plants makes a wonderful display of varied flowers and foliage despite the shady, albeit rich, conditions. Remember to incorporate paths and clearings in your plan to increase your enjoyment of the area and to provide access to all parts of the garden.

Orange hawkweed (*Hieracium brunneo-croceum*) is one of those plants that was originally introduced to our gardens but which has since escaped to the wild to become quite a common sight along roadsides, on waste ground and in hedgerows especially in England and Wales, The bright orange flowers with large yellow centres are a cheerful sight in midsummer, raised on long stalks as high as 20cm (8in).

Growing only to about 4m (13ft), the sloe or blackthorn (Prunus spinosa) is a good choice for small gardens and for hedgerows. The dark spiny stems produce a mass of snowy blossom in spring to be followed by green leaves in summer and dull blue-black berries in autumn, which are popular with birds, and for making sloe gin.

A small woodland makes a delightful feature complementary to all styles of garden, even a formal one. Plant a selection of trees and shrubs as a backdrop or boundary to the main scheme, linking it with the rest of the garden by using wild plants gradually giving way to more formal ones.

Tall Trees

Even smaller suburban gardens have room for a few tall trees – the 'canopy' of your woodland scheme – and they may be able to serve a practical as well as a decorative purpose. Columnar or conical evergreens like holly or Irish yew make fine all-year-round screening if grown close together. Others may be used as the focal point or backbone of your scheme in conjunction with smaller species and ground cover plants. If they grow too large they can always be coppiced – this is the ancient technique of cutting certain trees almost to ground level every ten to fifteen years. With some species such as willow or dogwood this produces fine, whippy, coloured stems which not only look attractive but are also useful for basket making and other crafts.

Shrubs and Smaller Trees

Until your taller trees have grown and matured it is the 'understorey' that will command most interest and provide

The common shrubby hazel (Corylus avallana) has been cultivated from the wild since early man used to grow it for coppicing in oak woods. It is also called cob-nut for the tasty nuts it produces in autumn, but the spring catkins are equally attractive.

adequate shade for your woodland flowers. Smaller trees and shrubs should be planted close enough together for their branches to be virtually entwined – allowing for paths and clearings, of course. Many of the smaller trees are quick growing and offer excellent garden value with attractive foliage, flowers and fruits; rowan for example, the fast-growing silver birch has a distinctive bark and fine foliage; while hawthorn has lovely green leaves, pretty summer blossom and red berries at the end of the year. Fast-growing ramblers like rose and bramble are an excellent way to create a temporary 'thicket' which can be cut back as the slower-growing, larger specimens begin to come into their own.

Awkward shady corners can be difficult to plant up but a lush selection of woodland plants will make a fine and flourishing display.

Prickly gorse or furze (Ulex europaeus) is a familiar heathland plant, and there are various types (including a dwarf variety) which flower at different times of the year. The spiny branches make this a good boundary plant; the massed flowers are a brilliant buttery yellow.

Ground-Cover Plants

Down on the woodland floor a fascinating variety of lovely plants flourish in the shady or semi-shady conditions beneath shrubs and trees. Even dense shade will support some of the prettiest plants like lily of the valley, exotic cyclamen and wood avens. Elsewhere allow a carpet of starry woodruff, glossy ground ivy or delicate violets to spread itself. Along the moist, shady edges of your woodland area an even greater variety of lovely wild flowers is possible: mostly perennial or biennial plants that have a quick spreading habit which makes them easy to maintain. You can easily choose a fine variety of types, contrasting fern's feathery fronds with green hellebore's strange foliage, or with the fleshy leaves of one of spring's earliest plants – lungwort (*Pulmonaria*) – with its distinctive spotted foliage and tall stems of flowers. There is something for every season here from the first spring snowdrops and narcissi – plant them *en masse* beneath trees and shrubs – to pretty spreading woodruff (*Galium odoratum*) and the purple-pink flowers of the water avens (*Geum rivale*), which will keep flowering into autumn.

As the leafy canopy of the taller trees develops, you will need to introduce further

*The familar onion aroma in damp woodland areas is produced by bright green ramsons (*Allium ursinum*) which make excellent ground cover at a height of around 40cm (16in). They grow from bulbs and are easily propagated by lifting and separating the bulbs.*

*Red campion (*Silene dioica*) is a useful yet attractive plant for shady places, and has a long flowering season. It grows to around 80cm (2½ft). Hybridizing with white campion produces a more pinkish flower.*

shade-tolerant species: hostas, *alchemilla mollis*, foxgloves and astilbes – all stunning and dramatic plants for your woodland edge area.

Mulching woodland wild flowers with leaf mould or chopped bark will get them off to a good start before trees are mature enough to do the job themselves.

Creating a Woodland

Careful preparation of the ground is always worth the time and trouble, saving much hard work weeding and replacing plants that have failed. The proposed area for your woodland should be thoroughly dug over and all perennial weeds eradicated. Ideally the ground should be ready for planting during the autumn; the trees are dormant and so better able to survive the shock of being moved, but the soil is still warm enough to encourage good root growth. Planting in winter is also possible if the ground is not frozen or waterlogged.

Young bare-rooted trees are preferable to large container-grown specimens. The larger trees may give more of an instantly mature look, but the young whips are guaranteed to overtake them in no more than five years. The only problem with bare-rooted trees is that they do not like being kept out of the soil too long. Help reduce any anguish by keeping the tree roots damp and by giving an extra good soaking just before planting. Gently tease out the rootball taking care not to damage the more delicate rootlets, then lower it gently into a hole dug slightly larger, but to the right depth for the tree to come to the same level in the ground as it was growing before. A layer of leaf mould or compost in the bottom of the hole will help the tree get off to a good start. The hole should be backfilled, making sure the roots are well-firmed, and then the tree watered thoroughly. A layer of mulch or a sheet of plastic (topped with bark chips) laid about 45cm (18in) around the stem of the tree will help suppress weeds and to keep in moisture. A newly planted tree must be watered well during its first year, particularly during dry weather. Where trees, shrubs and ground-cover plants will be competing for nutrition and moisture it might be a good idea to organize some kind of automatic watering system.

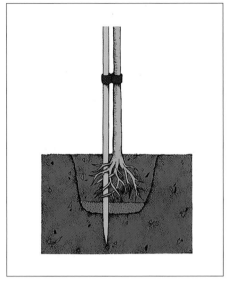

Saplings should be supported by a short stake and a proper tree tie to avoid wind damage.

Newly planted trees will also have to be correctly staked to prevent them suffering wind damage. You can buy special stake ties that allow the tree sufficient movement when the wind blows. Never use string or twine which tend to be too tight and distort the growth of the trunk and may even damage the tree permanently. It is also a good idea to put tree guards round the tree to protect it from rabbit and squirrel damage.

You can sow your ground-cover plants directly on to the soil beneath trees and shrubs in early spring although they will not flower until the following year. Alternatively, if the planted area is not a large one, you might use established plants for flowers the next season. Woodland plants enjoy a rich fertile soil and it may be necessary to mulch with organic matter such as bark chips for a few years until fallen leaves, bark and other tree debris have begun to establish an appropriate balance.

6 • PLANTS FOR DRY SUNNY AREAS

Many wild flowers enjoy an open sunny site and will do well in garden beds and borders or on grassy banks and stone walls. To get the most out of this lovely informal display, pack the plants in profusion: whether you are planning a completely natural mixture of shapes and colours or a mixture of wild and more cultivated species, the more you plant the better. You should not be able to see any bare patches of soil at all, which not only looks more attractive but helps reduce the burden of watering and weeding too.

Wildflower Walls and Patios

A large selection of wild flowers which have adapted to the harsh conditions of

Delicate alpine flowers are perfect for creating a miniature wildflower garden in a small trough or old sink. Stand it in a sunny part of the garden or on the patio.

Hillside and mountain species are perfect for brightening up a dry stone wall, as well as encouraging a variety of lizards, insects and other wildlife to breed and feed within its crevices.

mountain and cliffside are tough enough to grow in the dryest, stoniest parts of the garden making them extremely useful for brightening up paving or decorating old stone walls. These can .be made to look more interesting with a few such plants to soften their stony outlines: fleshy sedums, the mountain avens (*Dryas octopetala*) striking sea holly (*Eryngium maritimum*) or the fine silver-grey foliage of the aromatic sea wormwood (*Artemisia maritima*). Creeping wild plants can also do a good job softening the outlines of patio stones and slabs: creeping thymes and marjorams will add scent as well as pretty colour to your back yard when planted in the cracks between the pavers.

The coltsfoot (*Tussilago farfara*) is perfect for difficult stony areas of the garden, as in the wild it prefers barren, rather bare, spots and will even grow in shingle or gravel. The flowers are the predominant part of the plant growing around 25cm (10in) high on a thick scaly stem; they look like tiny yellow pompoms. Extract of the plant was once a popular remedy for coughs.

Alternatively, plan a proper rock or seaside garden on a rocky mound or in a sink or trough, growing pretty pink sea thrift, tiny alpine lady's mantle (*Alchemilla alpina*) or creeping wild thyme. Alpine wild flowers like plenty of sun and good drainage but adequate water too, especially during dry weather, so cover any bare patches of soil with chippings to help conserve moisture.

Sunny Banks

You often see wild flowers growing vigorously up a grassy bank or slope: on an incline such as this they receive plenty of sunshine and the drainage is good, conditions which suit many species well. The bank is a feature that can be usefully copied in our own gardens to add height and interest at eye level. If you don't already have something like it in the garden, you could build one from scratch, especially if you have a mound of soil left over from some kind of excavation such as new drains or a garden pool. Providing the soil is properly prepared and free from weeds as described on page 40, you can seed it with

*Delicate harebells (*Campanula rotundifolia*) are a late summer treat in dry grassy places such as banks and roadsides. The tiny bells are supported on slender stems and grow to a height of around 25cm (10in).*

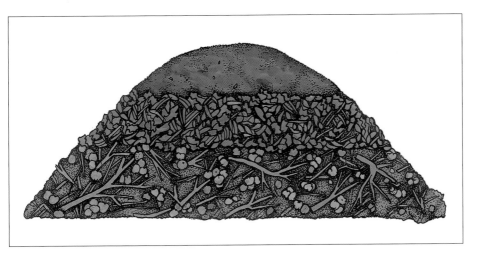

The subsoil from another garden feature such as a pond can be used to create a wildflower bank. If you do not have any spare subsoil, use woody garden compost like pruned branches, grass mowings and dead leaves; mound it up and allow to rot down to produce a bank of humus-rich soil.

one of the meadow flower mixes and enjoy a whole range of plants, from cowslips and clover to lady's bedstraw or delicate bird's-foot trefoil.

Many wild flowers prefer a chalky soil and this is easily accommodated by building a chalk bank and stocking it with such plants as wild thyme, wild carrot and pretty salad burnet. Build the bank out of chalk rubble – you don't need any soil – which has to be compacted so that it makes a better seed bed. It should not be any taller than 90cm (3ft), nor should the sides be excessively steep or it will look unnatural. What is important is that the bank should enjoy full sun. Suitable seeds can be sown directly into the soil.

Beds and Borders

Bedding and herbaceous plants can easily be replaced by wildflower species in your beds and borders to create a softer, more

Stately foxglove (*Digitalis purpurea*) with its large cluster of trumpet-like blooms is already a garden favourite, as it provides an excellent display of shape and colour towards the rear of beds and borders. Plants may grow as tall as 1.5m (5ft). In the wild it is a commonly seen woodland and hedgerow plant flowering right through the summer. The highly attractive flower spikes are usually purple with spotted detail, but there is also a white form. The plant is highly poisonous, the drug digitalis being extracted to treat heart disease. Foxgloves can be perennial or biennial.

Some wild flowers make excellent subjects for a sunny border, where they may be mingled with more cultivated species. Alternatively grow a selection of species together in a group or swathe to blend with a copse or woodland behind.

informal look. Growing them among a framework of shrubs, small trees and a few carefully selected garden plants, will reduce any maintenance tasks and give height and body to the feature. They look particularly good, however, grown in conjunction with old-fashioned cottage-garden flowers and herbs, which have the right kind of informal look and offer a wide range of soft colours.

Wild plants look best grown in happy abundance so do make sure the display is loosely arranged in swathes or blocks. Over the seasons, self-seeded plants and spreading perennials will tend to do their own thing, but selective weeding should bring a rough kind of order to the display. Try to keep taller varieties to the rear or centre of your planning scheme with ground-cover plants to soften the edges at the front. There is certainly plenty of choice of shape, size and colour: use them with pleasure as wild flowers rarely clash but live side by side in apparent harmony. Strong elements might include the unmistakable bright blooms of poppies, the nodding stems of purple foxgloves, spidery red greater knapweed, dark mullein, fascinating giant thistles or the great flower heads of angelica. More delicate forms for the front rows might include the tiny snapdragon flowers of common toadflax, pale blue harebells, musk-scented moschatel or star-studded purple saxifrage.

7 • POND, MARSH AND STREAM

A small natural pond is probably the most common wild plant feature to be found in our gardens. It is a desirable and practical option for virtually any size and style garden, and will even suit the patio; once installed it gives a great deal of pleasure in return for very little maintenance. A pond is an asset in itself: it adds light and movement to your garden scheme, while water plants, whether in the pool or growing in the damp margins, are quick and easy to grow producing a mature effect within a single season. Few garden features, let alone a wildflower one, can offer such variety and drama as a pond containing plants like the giant gunnera, spiky bulrushes and the calm, unreal beauty of water-lilies. Then there is the

fascinating range of wildlife which seems to appear as if drawn by a magnet: insects (such as stunning dragonflies), frogs and toads, fish and various birds, all flock to feed and breed. Even a small pond is important environmentally with so many acres of valuable wetlands disappearing annually.

A pond looks good planned in conjunction with other wildflower features such as a marsh, meadowland or woodland, and where plants can be used to merge one feature with the next. None of these features needs to be enormous – scale your ideas up or down according to how much space you have. Water features do need a little thought about where they are going to be sited. A sunny open site is ideal as nearby

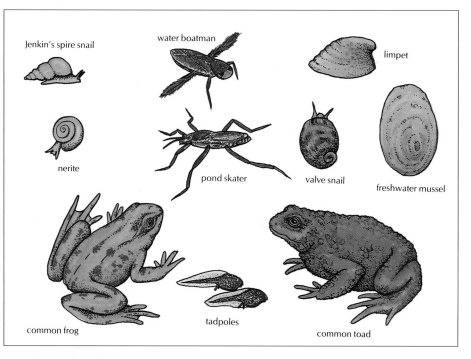

Jenkin's spire snail

water boatman

limpet

nerite

pond skater

valve snail

freshwater mussel

common frog

tadpoles

common toad

A pond or marsh garden attracts a wonderful variety of wildlife which comes to feed and drink, or to use the water or surrounding plants to nest and breed. As well as frogs, snails and insects, you might also expect small mammals like voles or even mink.

trees tend to be a nuisance, polluting the water with dropped leaves and, if they are positioned to the south and west, by casting unwelcome shade. Most wild water plants prefer plenty of sunshine to flourish. That said, a few trees or shrubs relatively near by – perhaps linked by a belt of suitable marsh and pool-edge plants like huge *Gunnera manicata*, elegant bamboo or spiky reeds and grasses – provide excellent cover for wildlife wishing to use the pool.

Often a dip or hollow will suggest where a pool might be sited and look perfectly natural; or else a damp area in the garden makes an excellent starting point for a marsh garden. A natural stream is a delightful feature bordered by all manner of charming wild flowers, and might be crossed by stepping stones or simple rustic bridges to create a lovely meandering boundary between other garden features.

A Wildlife Pond

Even a small informal pond can transform the garden into a far more interesting and exciting place. It is well worth the time and trouble to install, although any upheaval from installation can be minimized if you tackle the project sensibly. We have already discussed the best site for a sunken pool: it is essential that the feature looks perfectly natural in its setting, which is why an existing dip or hollow makes a good choice. Clever planting and choice of surrounding materials, or complementary adjoining features can all help your pond integrate more successfully with the rest of the garden.

The actual shape of your pond must be as natural-looking as possible; you can buy preformed informal shapes, but if you are creating your own style, stick to an irregular oval, kidney, or leg of mutton shape with gentle curves but no narrow inlets, which not only look wrong but hinder construction too. Gently sloping or shelved sides and shallows make it easier for small animals to use the pond and also offer the chance to grow an interesting selection of marginal plants. Any gradient should be less than 1:3 or the soil will slip down and settle on the bottom of the pool.

Size – and shape to some extent – will depend on the site available and generally

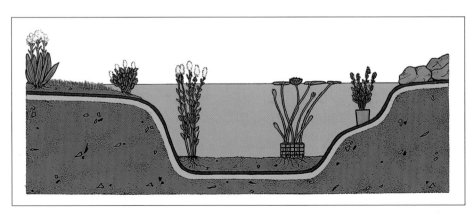

When constructing a natural pond you must allow a range of different depths from gently sloping shallows to a minimum depth of 80cm (2½ft). This will prevent part of the pond freezing over in winter so that fish can shelter.

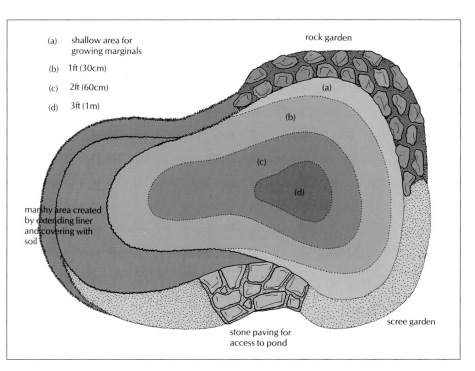

(a) shallow area for growing marginals

(b) 1ft (30cm)

(c) 2ft (60cm)

(d) 3ft (1m)

rock garden

(a)

(b)

(c)

(d)

marshy area created by extending liner and covering with soil

stone paving for access to pond

scree garden

A natural pond has a gently curving contour which can incorporate a variety of wetland habitats for plants and creatures, including deep water, shallows and areas of waterlogged soil for bog plants.

speaking you should make your pond as big as you dare for maximum enjoyment. Small pools are fine but bigger ones are more fun and can look great even in small gardens. A pond approximately 1.2–1.5sq m (13–16sq ft) with a minimum depth of about 75cm (2½ft) is a good average size if you are in doubt. The hardest part is digging the hole and this should be done with a mechanical digger unless the pond is particularly small. These may be hired by the day or weekend with or without an operator, depending on the size and type of machine. To make the most of hiring equipment such as this you should make sure the site is ready, that you have proper safe access and that you know where you are going to put

all the subsoil: if you are not using it elsewhere in the garden (to create another feature such as a rock garden or flowery bank), you may have to hire a skip too.

The ideal time to install a pool is in spring when there is not only a better chance of good weather, but, once in place, the water has a whole summer to warm up and the plants have a chance to become established before dying back. Begin by marking out the area using pegs and string or a length of hosepipe. This way you can keep adjusting the shape until you are happy it looks right. Cut the turf inside your shape with a spade and start rolling it back in strips. If you roll these up turf-side inwards and keep watered they can be used elsewhere in the garden.

A large natural pond can play host to a wide range of wildflower plants, from lovely lilies on the water's surface to plants like iris, fritillary and loosestrife around the banks.

Next, remove the topsoil and store this too; you might use it later for plants. Once the pond is roughly dug you can finish it by hand using a spirit-level to ensure the banks are level: place this on a straight piece of timber to span the width of the pool. Remember to incorporate a marginal shelf below the water's surface for positioning water-edge plants. Remove any sharp stones or sticks from the sides and bottom of the excavation and cover with a thin layer of sand about 5cm (2in) deep.

Lining Your Pond

There are various ways you can line a pond: the most natural way for large ponds is to compact the soil around the sides, in areas where the clay content in the soil is high enough to make a watertight bond; this is called clay puddling. Garden ponds used to be all lined with concrete – an effective if not easy process for the amateur – until the manufacture of polythene, PVC and butyl rubber provided better alternatives. Flexible pond liners mould themselves easily to the shape of the pond and are particularly suited to irregular informal styles. You can also buy preformed fibreglass liners complete with marginal shelf but these limit you to whatever shapes and sizes are in stock at your local water garden centre. To install one of these, you must excavate a hole slightly larger than your liner, lower the mould into position and backfill with soil taking care the liner remains level.

Flexible Liners

Flexible liners come in a choice of colours, mainly blue and black. Polythene and PVC are the less expensive types, but are not all very durable, splitting and discolouring after prolonged exposure to frosts and strong sunlight. Much tougher and long-lasting is butyl liner, but this is also more expensive. You can buy lining material in precut sheets or off the roll to whatever length you need. For large ponds, sections can be joined with a waterproof seal.

You must dig your hole as described above allowing an extra 20cm (8in) on the depth for the cushioning material necessary with flexible liners. When calculating how much lining material you need, allow a little extra for tucking over the top and anchoring under a suitable edging material, but any excess other than this is unnecessary since the liner stretches to fit. If the day is cool, placing the liner in a warm room until you are ready to fit it makes it a little more workable. Meanwhile you must line the hole with a suitable polypropylene lining material to protect the liner; old newspapers or carpet can be used if you are on a limited budget. Lay the liner loosely over the hole and anchor it round the edges with smooth boulders or similar non-sharp heavy weights. If you lay a hosepipe on the bottom of the pond and allow water to run in slowly, the weight of the water will pull the liner tightly into position. Help it along a little by smoothing out any creases and tucking any excess material away at the corners. If using tap-water wait a few days for the chlorine to evaporate before stocking with fish or plants.

Concrete liner

Mixed correctly concrete can be strong and durable and is particularly suited to formal-style and raised ponds, or where you may need to stand in the pond without ripping the liner with your boots. It can be used for informal wildlife pools providing the edges can be well disguised. The drawbacks are that it can be tricky to install if you haven't done much work with concrete before; also even with the appropriate additives there is

In England and the southern Scottish Borders large clumps of comfrey (*Symphytum officinale*) are a common sight wherever the ground is damp, for example along river banks, and in ditches and damp woodland areas. This native perennial grows to around 1m (3ft) high, making a dense clump of thick hairy leaves which have excellent healing qualities, giving comfrey its popular name of knitbone. The drooping keys of flowers can be mauve, white or pink. It grows easily, so makes an excellent taller plant for damp areas of the garden. It has a long flowering season throughout the summer.

a risk of frost damage where winter conditions are cold. The hole must be shuttered with timbers – soaped for easy removal afterwards – and the concrete poured in as quickly and evenly as possible. The pond can be filled with water as soon as the concrete has hardened to the touch although in fact it will continue to harden over a very long period. You will not be able to stock with fish or plants until the water has been changed two or three times over a period of three to four weeks to remove any poisonous lime that may have leached out of the concrete.

Clay Puddling

If your soil has a high clay content you can puddle the sides naturally to create the ideal environment for your water-loving wild flowers. You can buy a type of clay specially

A small pond could be suggested by sinking a small waterproof container, such as a tub, in the garden and surrounding it with an interesting selection of water-loving plants like ferns and reeds.

recommended for pond and reservoir use but this might work out very expensive over large areas. The wet clay can be puddled with your hands in small pools but larger ones will probably require skilled use of a mechanical digger. Trial and error may be required to get the technique right.

Miniature Ponds

If space is really limited or excavation not practical – if you are intending to move home, for example, or have only a roof or balcony garden – a small free-standing container might provide an excellent wildlife pond in miniature. An old sink, a half-barrel or indeed any waterproof tub or container might display a few small aquatic plants, a miniature water-lily and contain fish or frogs. Make sure your chosen container has

not been waterproofed with anything poisonous, then place approximately 6–10cm (3–4in) of soil or sand and gravel in the bottom and allow to settle.

Pond Surrounds

Unless your pond is in a self-contained tub or urn, disguising the exposed edges of your lining material and integrating the feature with its surroundings is particularly important for a natural pond. This is easily done if you observe how it looks in the wild: a grassy bank, rocky boulders or a gently sloping pebble beach, together with a selection of pool-side plants are ideal for encouraging a wide selection of wildlife to drink, feed, bathe and nest. A pond can often be integrated successfully with another wildflower feature such as a flowery

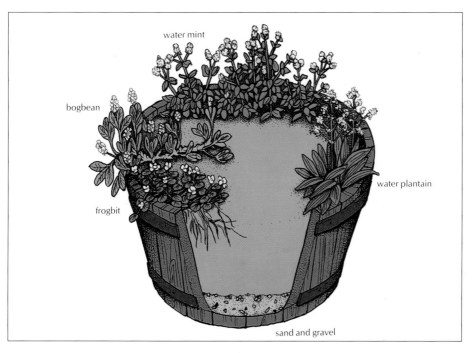

You can create a miniature wildlife pond for the patio using a watertight half-barrel, pot or similar container. Choose the smaller varieties of water plants with tiny leaves and miniature flowers: an oxygenator such as water milfoil is a good idea too. With a few stones or boulders in the bottom you will be surprised at the snails and insects that find their way there.

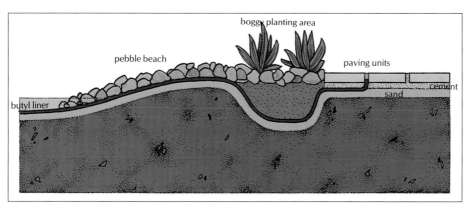

A pebble beach is a very natural and attractive way to finish off the edges of a wildlife pond or pool. Run the pebbles right into the shallows to allow small mammals and birds easy access to the water.

You can use a waterfall to link a rocky wildflower or alpine feature with a natural pond; this is a useful way to use the excavated subsoil too. It can be tricky to get a waterfall to look natural but if you study how the rocks lie and where the water flows in the wild, trial and error should achieve a successful result.

meadow, a marsh garden or a rocky alpine outcrop complete with waterfall.

It is not easy to create a successful waterfall, but trial and error and close attention to how the rocks should lie ought to produce convincing results. Lining behind the rocks with flexible liner prevents loss of water down the back of the stones. Frogs, toads and other small mammals will enjoy living in the crevices between the rocks while the falling water (powered by a small submersible pump in the pool below) usefully oxygenates the water.

For a semi-formal look, you might incorporate flat paving stones to project over the edge of the pond, or an arrangement of bricks or slabs. These will not only provide somewhere dry to sit and observe the wildlife, but also a place where some creatures might bask in the sunshine – plus a possible visual link with other garden features, of course.

Marsh Garden

There are many advantages to the marsh or bog garden: for one thing, there is no digging which makes it quick and easy to install. The kind of plants which grow there are showy and dramatic (for wild plants) which guarantees a good display; and it is an ideal way to grow these lush water-loving plants if you have children, as there is no danger of standing water. All you need to create your own marsh or bog is an area of poorly drained, waterlogged land that you could probably do nothing else with without installing expensive land drains; or, if you lack space, a container as small as a barrel stood on the patio. The alternative is to lay a piece of punctured flexible pool liner over a slight hollow no more than 40cm (15in) deep. A layer of pebbles about 8cm (3in) deep should be sufficient for drainage, topped with a rich moist soil. The

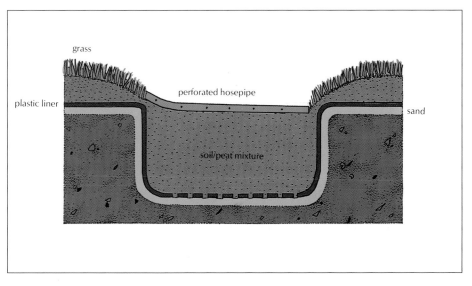

A marsh or wetland involves no digging and is easily created by laying down a perforated plastic or rubber liner on a layer of sand or pebbles for good drainage. A trickling or punctured hose-pipe will keep the area damp in hot weather.

A small stream needs a concealed water pump to circulate the water, but can be host to a lovely and varied arrangement of lush water plants.

area must be kept damp; laying a hosepipe in the bottom during construction means a constant trickle can be maintained in dry weather. Alternatively, the marsh might form part of a larger wildlife pond and act as a kind of overflow facility.

A stream makes an excellent boundary or way of dividing one part of the garden from another – maybe a formal area from a wildflower feature. Bridges can provide access from one part to another.

Large areas of waterlogged land could also be seeded with a wildflower wetland meadow mixture, which includes plants like ragged robin (*Lychnis flos-cuculi*), yellow loosestrife (*Lysimachia vulgaris*) or the delicate water avens. The ground will have to be prepared as for meadows (page 24), making sure there are no perennial weeds. The area should dry out on the surface in summer sealing the moisture beneath, and should be scythed down in autumn.

Streams

A natural stream meandering along its rocky bed and bordered by all manner of pretty water-loving wild flowers makes a delightful feature. Crossed by simple rustic bridges or stepping-stones, a stream can be a useful device for defining a boundary or dividing one area of the garden from another, making

Rocks and boulders soon give a natural appearance to a man-made stream, interplanted with suitable stream and poolside plants.

the route between them instantly more interesting. In the wild a stream changes course when it meets an object of greater resistance such as a rock or boulder, which should give some clue as to the general shape and design. It need not have any water in it at all, but rather be a stony 'dry stream' in the manner of the traditional oriental gardens – a good selection of lush water-loving plants like ferns, marsh marigolds and skunk cabbage along its banks will be all the suggestion it needs. If you do wish to introduce running water, the base of the stream will have to be lined behind the stones and the water moved by means of an electric water pump.

Water Plants

After a couple of years you will find that any natural pond – even a large one – will be fully equipped, as if by magic, with native plants and a wide selection of wildlife, from fish and snails to insects and small mammals. Many just seek out the water; others arrive as eggs or seeds brought on the bills and beaks of visiting birds. However, if you wish to speed up nature a little, a bucket of mud from a friend or neighbour's pool will introduce plenty of natural wildlife; while plants can be purchased from your local water garden specialists or grown from cuttings begged from or swapped with friends. Water plants tend to be difficult to grow from seed. You need to look out for the kind of plants you would see growing in the wild: you don't need showy hybrids and extravagant variations to create a bold display, as many pond and marsh plants have striking foliage; they are also so prolific that you don't need many plants to make a fine show, even within a single season.

A selection of oxygenating plants will be useful for keeping a good ecological balance in the water; they help prevent it turning a murky green too, although if this common problem persists, you should consider installing a small electrically run filter. In larger ponds try a bale of straw suspended in the water to act as a natural filter. Oxygenators are pretty but they can grow a

A natural pond can support a wonderful variety of moisture-loving plants, not just in the water or on the marginal shelf, but in the moist soil close to the water too.

little too well, so keep them in check if you don't want them to take over the pond. You will need one oxygenating plant for each 1,000 sq cm (1 sq ft) of water. Water milfoil (*Myriophyllum*) has delicate white flowers; the water violet (*Hottonia palustris*) is particularly lovely, making a carpet of lilac flowers with yellow centres. If you plant them in special open-mesh containers anchored to the bottom of the pond with a pebble, they can be removed if necessary for maintenance. Most pond owners like to grow at least one water-lily; they need quite a lot of space so only the larger ponds will be able to support more than one type.

Choose one of the less fancy hybridized types and allow a depth of at least 15cm (6in); the plants are grown in meshed containers and stood on blocks or bricks in the water to make sure the familiar disc-shaped leaves and lotus flowers rest on the surface. There are also dwarf varieties available which are suitable for container ponds.

Moving towards the edge of the pond there are some plants that enjoy the water-submerged soil of the shallows and will grow happily on the marginal shelf: for example galingale (*cyperus*) with its showy umbrella stems, or the flowery blue carpet produced by the water forget-me-not (*Myosotis scorpoides*). Other species thrive in the damp rich area close to the water's surface of a pond, marsh or stream: the flowering rush (*Butomus umbellatus*), tall purple-flowered loosestrife (*Lythrum salicaria*), golden yellow marsh marigolds (*Caltha palustris*) with their waxen blooms or the elegant flag iris.

There are many types and colours of water-lily, including a dwarf variety suitable for the smallest pool.

8 • MAINTENANCE

Nature may look after her own in the wild but in the wildflower garden careful, if unobtrusive, control is necessary to keep the area looking at its best. You are aiming at a natural informal effect, not a tangle of weeds. That does not mean to say wild flowers require tedious maintenance once established, provided you took the trouble to eliminate all perennial weeds before you started planting. On the contrary, if you can keep up with a few seasonal chores, you will be rewarded by a charming and seemingly effortless display.

Weeding can be the biggest chore although even this is not a problem in grass and meadowland where seasonal cutting and the vigorous nature of other plants keeps weeds in check. You will soon learn which plants to leave and which to remove in other wildflower areas. Many will be self-seeded wild flowers so providing they are attractive and that one species is not beginning to swamp all the other plants around it, you may as well leave them be. There are some perennials which spread by means of creeping roots, for example buttercups, ground elder and couch grass, and these can be a real menace. You are advised to remove as many of these as you can, digging out every tiny piece of root and burning it. If you do want to be strict about which flowers you have in your garden, buy yourself a good weed identification book.

If you have given plants the conditions they prefer in the wild they should not need regular watering. Until the ground is fully covered and plants have matured, a mulch of wood chips or gravel helps reduce moisture loss from the soil. Ponds, streams and marsh gardens may need top-up facilities during dry spells; remember to use rainwater or tap-water that has been allowed to stand to avoid adding harmful chlorine. You do not generally need to fertilize most wildflower features. Most prefer an impoverished soil; others, such as marsh or woodland plants, tend to be enriched by organic material supplied by surrounding plants. If the soil is too sandy, chalky or clay-bound for a particular group of plants you might try adding a little organic compost such as spent mushroom compost, to improve its natural balance. It is plants grown in the limited environment of a container that usually require additional nutrients. Use liquid seaweed feeds rather than chemical products which seem to encourage uneven growth and pest attack.

As a rule, wild plants do not seem to attract the same kind of problems of aphid and pest attack as their more hybridized cousins, encouraging as they do a wide range of predatory insects such as ladybirds and lacewings. If things do get out of balance you might try natural pesticides such as derris or pyrethrum, but take care that you use these only in the evening as they can be harmful to ladybirds, bees and fish.

While flowery meadows release you from the twice-a-week summer burden of mowing the lawn, they still require mowing at the appropriate time or they will revert to being mainly grass. Timing will depend on whether you have a spring- or summer-flowering meadow (see page 26). Most shrubs and trees only require trimming and pruning to keep them in check. The exception is the wildlife hedgerow which must be cut back annually once it has matured to prevent it growing too thick and tall. Hedge plants should not be trimmed too formally; do not worry if a trim looks a little severe — it will grow back with renewed vigour in spring. In the country, established hedges that have become maybe a little gappy are sometimes 'layed' or pleached. This involves splitting stems almost to the ground and weaving them horizontally to create a good stock-proof barrier.

The woodland wild garden could not be simpler to maintain: fallen leaves can be left to rot down to create valuable compost to feed woodland wild flowers. Trees may

Wild daffodils, allowed to spread themselves, transform a rough grassy area in spring, yet leave time for flowering plants to flourish in summer.

need pruning to size in smaller gardens but even fallen branches and rotting logs can be left where they lie to encourage interesting insects such as beetles, and fungi. Allowed to maintain this natural balance, feeding and watering will not be necessary and woodland plants will propagate themselves quite readily. To start them off, a woodland seed mixture or selected seed of individual plants might be introduced the first spring or autumn after planting your saplings. Bulbs and pot grown plants or plantlets should not be planted until the trees are at least 1.5m (5ft) tall.

Ponds and marsh gardens also require very little attention once established. Autumn is perhaps the busiest time when rampant plants require cutting back and ponds need to be kept clear from falling leaves by netting or dredging. Unless the pond is a large one with a strong healthy ecological system in operation, leaves rot and release poisonous gases, polluting the water. Plants are easier to maintain if they have been planted in individual containers or mesh baskets which can be lifted for treatment. This is also the best time to consider repairs if the liner is damaged or if the pond requires a general overhaul. At the end of summer plants and wildlife become dormant so will not be quite so disturbed.

Pests and diseases are not usually a problem with ponds; if you do see any aphids munching your water-lilies, hose them off into the water where they will be eaten by fish. Some species of fish and snails will eat your plants: get rid of them at once. With larger ponds, wildfowl can sometimes be a problem, greedily gobbling up all your wild flowers. You will have to decide whether you prefer to have the fowl or the plants and act accordingly: birds will be discouraged by any lack of cover and nesting places.

Murky water can sometimes be a problem in summer: this is due to an excess of sunshine encouraging algae to be over-active. Oxygenating plants such as water milfoil and frogbit are nature's answer; alternatively you could install a small water filter or a slow-release chemical bag available from garden centres. A bale of straw sometimes works as a natural filter in large ponds (*see* page 56).

Winter is only a problem if your pond is shallow and you are worried that any fish will not survive. Never try to break ice by smashing it – this stuns any wildlife and it refreezes almost immediately anyway. A water heater could be the answer in small ponds and is relatively inexpensive to run; or you might try floating a plastic ball in the corner of small ponds to prevent the ice exerting any pressure on the sides. Frost and sun damage is possible: if this occurs the feature will have to be drained after carefully transferring plants and wildlife to a temporary refuge. Both flexible liners and concrete can be repaired; take care you do not cause further damage to rubber- and plastic-lined pools by wearing boots in the bottom.

Species daffodils look delightful planted en masse as a spring feature in a meadow or woodland area where more elaborate cultivated varieties would look out of place. Plant in blocks or swathes – never individually – for maximum effect.

A carpet of shiny dark-green, almost arrow-shaped, leaves and bright yellow flowers so glossy they look as though they have been varnished, is a common sight in spring throughout woods and hedgerows. The lesser celandine (*Ranunculus ficaria*) is a native perennial plant growing about 20cm (8in) high; its mat-forming habit makes it difficult to eradicate once established. There is also a greater celandine (*Chelidonium majus*) which is much taller – about 75cm (29.5in) high – and which has smaller clusters of yellow flowers and leaves more like a chrysanthemum. Celandines are commonly seen along roadsides and on waste ground.

Spring

● Sow seed for next year's plants and plant out pot-grown specimens for flowering this summer.
● Keep an eye on wildflower beds and borders, weeding out any unwanted weed seedlings and thinning out self-seeded plants.
● Mow late summer-flowering meadows.
● Leave spring-flowering bulbs to set seed and die down.

Summer

● Mow flowering lawns and spring- and early summer-flowering meadows.
● Check that marsh and pond features have not dried up during hot weather and top up with water where necessary.
● Look out for any pest infestation on wildflower plants or water-lilies and treat immediately (before it takes hold) by spraying with water or a soapy solution.

Water-lilies can be prone to beetle and aphid infestation: the best non-chemical cure is to hose the insects off into the water where they will be eaten by fish.

The mountain or hedgerow crane's-bill (Geranium pyrenaicum) *grows on waste ground and in hedgerows, producing attractive purple/pink flowers through the summer.*

● Slugs and snails may be part of life's rich pattern but they can destroy foliage plants. Going out after dark with a torch and bucket is the non-chemical treatment. Encouraging frogs and hedgehogs is the easiest option.

● Mulch areas of soil still bare with wood chips or gravel to help retain moisture.

● If you see fish in your pond coming to the surface and gasping for breath, oxygen levels have dropped. Remove the top couple of inches and replace with fresh, unchlorinated water.

Autumn

● Sow seed of annual meadow and corn-field species for next year. Also wild flowers for beds and borders.

● Plant trees, shrubs and spring-flowering bulbs.

● Mow or cut late summer-flowering meadows.

● Cut back and thin out or divide rampant water plants. Clean out the pond if damaged or silted up, having first removed any plants and fish and drained off the water.

Winter

● You can continue planting trees and shrubs so long as the ground is not frozen or waterlogged.

● Prune hedgerow plants and cut back any young trees to shape. Look out for young saplings and offshoots and remove these immediately before they spoil the shape of your hedge.

● Check ponds and streams during extreme cold weather: pumps that run moving water features will need overhauling; keeping them running prevents the water freezing so quickly.

● Knock snow from trees and shrubs to prevent the weight breaking branches.

PROTECTED PLANTS

The following wild plants are protected under the terms of the Wildlife and Countryside Act 1981 in the United Kingdom. This forbids any part of the plant to be uprooted or picked, or seed to be collected. New specimens are always being added so check in *The British Red Data Book 1: Vascular Plants*, published by the Royal Society for Nature Conservation. The fines for disturbing or taking seed from any of these plants are considerable. It is an offence to uproot any wild plant whether it is on this list or not.

Schedule of Protected Plants

Common name	Scientific name	Common name	Scientific name
Adder's-tongue spearwort	*Ranunculus ophioglossifolius*	Monkey orchid	*Orchis simia*
Alpine catchfly	*Lychnis alpina*	Norwegian sandwort	*Arenaria norvegica*
Alpine gentian	*Gentiana nivalis*	Oblong woodsia	*Woodsia ilvensis*
Alpine sow-thistle	*Cicerbita alpina*	Oxtongue broomrape	*Orobanche loricata*
Alpine woodsia	*Woodsia alpina*	Perennial knawel	*Scleranthus perennis*
Bedstraw broomrape	*Orobanche caryophyllacea*	Plymouth pear	*Pyrus cordata*
		Purple spurge	*Euphorbia peplis*
Blue heath	*Phyllodoce caerulea*	Red helleborine	*Cephalanthera rubra*
Brown galingale	*Cyperus fuscus*	Ribbon-leaved water-	*Alisma gramineum*
Cheddar pink	*Dianthus gratianopolitanus*	plantain	
		Rock cinquefoil	*Potentilla rupestris*
Childling pink	*Petrorhagia nanteuilii*	Rock sea-lavender (two rare species)	*Limonium paradoxum*
			Limonium recurvum
Diapensia	*Diapensia lapponica*	Rough marsh-mallow	*Althaea hirsuta*
Dickie's bladder-fern	*Cystopteris dickieana*	Round-headed leek	*Allium sphaerocephalon*
Downy woundwort	*Stachys germanica*	Sea knotgrass	*Polygonum maritimum*
Drooping saxifrage	*Saxifraga cernua*		
Early spider-orchid	*Ophrys sphegodes*	Sickle-leaved hare's-ear	*Bupleurum falcatum*
Fen orchid	*Liparis loeselii*	Small Alison	*Alyssum alyssoides*
Fen violet	*Viola persicifolia*	Small hare's-ear	*Bupleurum baldense*
Field cow-wheat	*Melampyrum arvense*	Snowdon lily	*Lloydia serotina*
		Spiked speedwell	*Veronica spicata*
Field eryngo	*Eryngium campestre*	Spring gentian	*Gentiana verna*
Field wormwood	*Artemisia campestris*	Starfruit	*Damasonium alisma*
Ghost orchid	*Epipogium aphyllum*	Starved wood-sedge	*Carex depauperata*
Greater-yellow-rattle	*Rhinanthus serotinus*	Teesdale sandwort	*Minuartia stricta*
Jersey cudweed	*Gnaphalium luteoalbum*	Thistle broomrape	*Orobanche reticulata*
Killarney fern	*Trichomanes speciosum*	Triangular club-rush	*Scirpus triquetrus*
		Tufted saxifrage	*Saxifraga cespitosa*
Lady's slipper	*Cypripedium calceolus*	Water germander	*Teucrium scordium*
		Whorled solomon's-seal	*Polygonatum verticillatum*
Late spider-orchid	*Ophrys fuciflora*		
Least-lettuce	*Lactuca saligna*	Wild cotoneaster	*Cotoneaster integerrimus*
Limestone woundwort	*Stachys alpina*		
Lizard orchid	*Himantoglossum hircinum*	Wild gladiolus	*Gladiolus illyricus*
Military orchid	*Orchis militaris*	Wood calamint	*Calamintha sylvatica*

GLOSSARY

Acid   The term used to describe soil or compost with a pH lower than 7.

Alkaline   The term used to describe soil or compost with a pH higher than 7, usually indicating a high lime content.

Alpine   A plant whose natural habitat is a thin-soiled, rocky terrain in harsh mountain regions and which is therefore ideally suited to rock or gravel gardens.

Annual   A plant that germinates, grows, blooms, sets seed and dies within a single year.

Biennial   Plant that germinates, grows, blooms, sets seed and dies within a two year period.

Bog   Area of waterlogged land, usually very acidic, suitable for plants which prefer their roots to be in permanently moist soil.

Broadcast   To sow or scatter seed over the ground instead of planting it in drills or rows.

Bulb   A plant storage organ containing food to carry the plant through its dormant phase, comprising fleshy leaves or a swollen leaf base.

Bulbils   Small bulbs found clustered at the base of some plants which can be detached and grown into full size plants.

Calcareous   Soil or compost containing a large percentage of chalk or lime and therefore alkaline.

Calcifuge   A plant that will not tolerate a soil with high lime content.

Chalk   The common name of the chemical compound calcium carbonate, identical (chemically) to limestone. It is usually applied to acid soil or compost as hydrated lime to increase its pH level.

Clay   A soil or compost comprising a mixture of fine sand and wet, sticky alumina. It is sticky to work when wet and dries to a hard cracked pan. However, when made more workable by the addition of organic material it is very fertile.

Conifer   A tree bearing cones.

Corm   Plant storage organ comprising a thickened underground stem.

Deciduous   Plant that loses its leaves before winter.

Evergreen   Term applied to any plant which loses and replaces its leaves gradually throughout the year so that foliage appears to be unchanged.

Exotic   Any plant not indigenous to the country in which it is growing. One that is unable to naturalize.

Ground cover   Dense, low-growing shrubby plants that produce a carpet effect of leaves and flowers.

Habit   The size and manner of growth of a plant, for example 'upright', 'creeping' etc.

Half-hardy   Term applied to winter-tender plants that require protection during the colder months.

Hedgerow   A hedge, usually made up of several wild species and sometimes incorporating a bank or ditch.

The beautifully elegant blooms of the giant bellflower can be seen in woodland and hedgerow areas where they grow to around 3ft (1m) high. They are a member of the Campanula *family.*

Herbaceous Term applied to any plant which makes soft sappy growth rather than the woody growth of a tree or shrub.

Humus Well-rotted organic matter used as a soil-building fertilizer.

Hybrid A cross between plants of different species, usually engineered to refine particular features.

Indigenous Term applied to a plant that is native to the area where it is growing.

Limestone Naturally occurring rock producing a surface soil with a high pH (that is, an alkaline soil). Chemically limestone is identical to chalk, both being calcium carbonate.

Marginal Term applied to plants which grow in the shallows at the edge of a pool or pond.

Marsh Area of land that is waterlogged at all times.

Moraine Bed of small stones or grit watered from below and particularly suitable for growing alpine plants.

Native Term applied to any plant that occurs naturally in its locality or country.

Naturalize To grow plants under conditions as close as possible to those found in their natural habitat; imported plants can be naturalized by allowing them to self-seed and establish themselves in the wild.

Oxygenators Term applied to plants which grow in or under the water and which give off significant levels of oxygen.

Perennial Plant which lives and flowers for a number of years.

Pleach Technique by which hedgerow saplings are split, bent and staked to shorten and thicken the hedge.

Raceme An unbranched flower spike with the flowers carried on equal-length stalks.

Rhizome An underground stem, usually growing horizontally, which produces shoots some distance from the parent plant.

Rootball Cluster of plant roots and soil.

Runner A plant shoot that roots at intervals along its length.

Species Group of plants that share the

Foxgloves look wonderful planted in a mass of purple flower spikes growing on a grassy bank, as well as hiding coyly in shady woodland areas.

same characteristics and which will interbreed.

Tap root Main, straight root of a plant, thicker at the top than at the base, from which the subsidiary rootlets grow.

Toxic Poisonous.

Variegated Foliage marked with contrasting coloured spots, stripes or blotches due to some mutation such as a benign virus or mineral deficiency.

Variety Group of plants within a species; or a plant with particularly distinctive characteristics.

Vernalization Technique by which seeds or bulbs are repeatedly exposed to low temperatures to imitate a natural winter and encourage germination or flowering.

INDEX